Contributors

Tricia Copeland
Nzondi
Lynda Williams
Kristina Rienzi
Catalina Paris
Charles Michael Austin, ED.D.
Bjorn Leesson
Candace MacPhie
Ann Charles & Sam Lucky
Alnoor Fadhl Alnoor
Albert Seligman
Alexander Alten
T. C. Weber
Steven Blows
Lee Cherry
Laurie Jame
G.T. DÍPÈ
Cinda Gault
D. J. O'Brien
Alan Chan

Review Tales
A Book Magazine For Indie Authors

Founder & Editor in Chief: S. Jeyran Main
Publisher: Review Tales Publishing & Editing Services
Print & Distribution: Ingram Spark
Designs: Pexels
ISBN 978-1-988680-70-5 (Paperback)
ISBN 978-1-988680-71-2 (Digital)
www.jeyranmain.com
For all inquiries, please contact us directly.

Photo Credits from Pexels:
nunzdy-17654216
jovanvasiljevic-20556794
omerderinyar-15366308
majesticaljasmin-8506600

A BOOK MAGAZINE FOR INDIE AUTHORS REVIEW TALES

Editor's Note

Welcome to the Summer 2025 edition of the Book Review Magazine—our 7th issue, and what a journey it's been! With each release, we celebrate the written word, the art of thoughtful critique, and the beauty of the community built around books.

Summer is a season of warmth, movement, and reflection. It's the perfect time to slow down with a good read or discover something unexpected that stays with you long after the last page. In this edition, we've gathered reviews and features that honor the voices of authors from all walks of life—those who write to uplift, challenge, inspire, or to tell a story only they can tell.

We're excited to bring you a vibrant collection of insights this season that don't just evaluate books but explore the heart behind them. Whether you're here as a longtime reader, a past contributor, or someone new to our pages, we hope you feel welcomed, valued, and inspired.

Don't hesitate to reach out if you've been thinking about having your book featured in an upcoming issue. We'd love to hear from you and learn more about the stories you have to share.

Thank you for turning these pages with us, issue after issue. Your support makes this community possible. So you can find your favorite reading spot, settle in, and let the summer stories unfold.

With gratitude and excitement,

Jeyran Main

Editor-in-Chief
Book Review Magazine

SUMMER 2025 | ISSUE 07

BOOK REVIEWS

Review Tales is thrilled to have reached the milestone of over 2000 book reviews. With this extensive experience, we've had the privilege of exploring a vast range of literature. Our reviews are always impartial and thoughtfully crafted to highlight authors' strengths while inspiring them to keep creating. For this summer issue, we've handpicked exceptional book reviews to feature.

TO APPLY FOR A BOOK REVIEW VISIT
WWW.JEYRANMAIN.COM

Book Reviews

TO BE A FAE BY TRICIA COPELAND

LIPSTICK ASYLUM BY NZONDI

THE BEAUTY AND THE HELL OF IT BY LYNDA WILLIAMS

WINTER ROAD BY KRISTINA RIENZI

THE MIDNIGHT ROSE BY CATALINA PARIS

HOW TO FIND WORK FOR THE REST OF YOUR LIFE BY CHARLES MICHAEL AUSTIN, ED.D.

RUNE OF WHISPERS BY BJORN LEESSON

HELLO I AM HERE BY CANDACE MACPHIE

CAN'T RIDE AROUND IT BY ANN CHARLES & SAM LUCKY

EXODUS FROM SUDAN BY ALNOOR FADHL ALNOOR

THE AMERICAN WEEKLY COVERS OF EDMUND DULAC BY ALBERT SELIGMAN

IGNITION BY ALEXANDER ALTEN

THE OTHERS BY T. C. WEBER

TALES OF THE FORTHCOMING BY STEVEN BLOWS

THE UNIQUE FRIENDSHIP OF GROVER & STEVE BY LEE CHERRY

SELF-MOTIVATION MIND SET BY LAURIE JAMES

RUNNIN' NO MORE BY G.T. DÍPÈ

A SMALL COMPASS BY CINDA GUALT

WYVERN (DARK LAIR TRILOGY: BOOK ONE) BY D. J. O'BRIEN

ABUNDANCE BY ALAN CHAN

TO BE A FAE
Tricia Copeland

Reviewer: Jeyran Main

To Be a Fae by Tricia Copeland is a richly imagined and emotionally charged young adult fantasy that draws readers into the magical and perilous world of Queen Titania. As darkness creeps across the enchanted realms, Titania must protect her people, confront inner demons, and uphold a fragile peace rapidly slipping through her fingers. Brimming with court intrigue, ancient prophecies, and the rising tide of spiritual corruption, this novel blends high fantasy with intimate personal stakes.

Titania is at the story's heart—a young and complex queen grappling with the weight of leadership, the pain of personal loss, and gnawing uncertainty about her destiny. As thefts, betrayals, and whispers of ancient threats emerge from the shadows, Titania is thrust into a mystery that challenges her ability to rule and the very soul of her kingdom. Alongside a close-knit group of companions, she must uncover truths long buried and make decisions that will echo throughout the magical realms.

Copeland's worldbuilding is a true highlight. Her vivid descriptions breathe life into the fae world, from glittering festival markets and enchanted kitchens to sacred soul rings and tense military councils. Every element of the setting feels purposeful and immersive. The magic here isn't just decoration—it's deeply entwined with the characters' lives, choices, and histories, enriching the narrative with layers of meaning.

Titania is a heroine who lingers in the mind long after the final page. She is fierce, deeply human, and unwavering in her commitment to her people—even when haunted by grief and doubt. Her journey is not only a quest to preserve peace but also one of self-discovery. Supporting characters like Isla, Makani, DJ, and Grant add humor, wisdom, and emotional depth to the story, each bringing their own strengths to the fight against the encroaching shadows.

What sets To Be a Fae apart is its exploration of themes such as mental health, generational trauma, identity, and the unifying power of hope. The magical stakes are high, but the emotional resonance remains rooted in universal human experience.

Perfect for Sarah J. Maas and Holly Black fans, To Be a Fae is a beautifully crafted fantasy tale that delivers spectacle and heart. It is a story of resilience, love, and the strength to protect peace in a world on the brink of war.

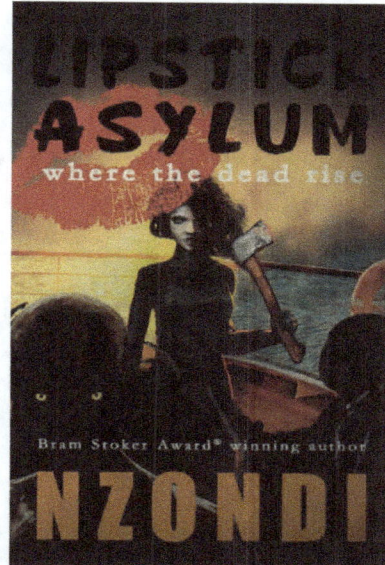

LIPSTICK ASYLUM
Nzondi

Reviewer: Jeyran Main

Lipstick Asylum by Nzondi (Ace Antonio Hall) is a genre-bending thrill ride that fuses horror, necromancy, and coming-of-age grit into a wildly original tale set aboard the world's eeriest cruise ship. Smart, funny, and bursting with attitude, the novel follows Cozy Coleman, an 18-year-old necromancer with a sharp tongue and a sharper edge. She makes her living raising the dead—until one high-profile resurrection goes gruesomely wrong.

Cozy, alongside her best friends Jess and Squiggy, boards the "Sea Queen," a floating hotel of horror-themed delights and undead spectacles. But what begins as a job quickly devolves into a nightmare as a strange illness spreads among passengers and a celebrity's zombie husband winds up headless — courtesy of the widow herself. With malfunctioning ceremonies, creepy zombie nuns, mysterious military figures, and a body count on the rise, Cozy must navigate a ship full of ghouls, secrets, and betrayal.

Nzondi's writing crackles with voice and energy. Cozy is a fiercely modern protagonist — brash and vulnerable beneath her snark. Her voice is unforgettable, layering slang, sarcasm, and sincerity. The dialogue is witty, the pacing relentless, and the horror is both campy and chilling, often within the same scene.

But Lipstick Asylum is more than a supernatural thrill ride. It touches on themes of grief, trauma, identity, and resilience. Cozy's heartbreak over the loss of her boyfriend and her complex relationship with necromancy anchor the story in real emotional stakes. Her bond with Jess is particularly moving, showcasing a fierce sisterhood that holds the narrative together even as chaos unfolds.

The setting — a cruise ship turned necromantic spectacle — is vividly imagined, blending Hawaiian nightlife with macabre theatrics. Nzondi leans into the absurd and theatrical while never losing sight of the human drama at its core.

Fans of Buffy the Vampire Slayer, Warm Bodies, or The Fifth Wave will find Lipstick Asylum a refreshing take on YA horror. It's bold, funny, culturally rich, and unafraid to be messy and real.

In short, this isn't your average zombie tale. Lipstick Asylum is undead fiction with a pulse — raw, wild, and impossible to put down.

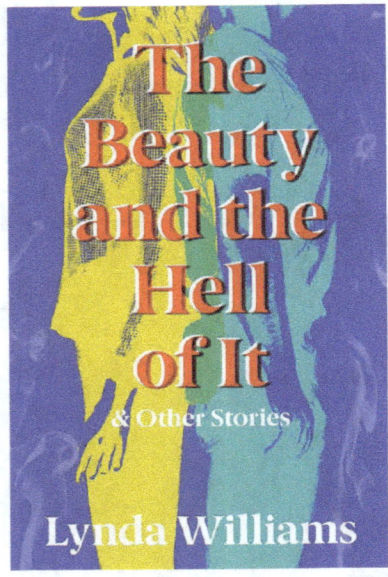

THE BEAUTY AND THE HELL OF IT & OTHER STORIES

Lynda Williams

Reviewer: Jeyran Main

Lynda Williams' The Beauty and the Hell of It is a fierce, unflinching, and unforgettable collection of short stories that lays bare the emotional landscapes of women navigating grief, motherhood, betrayal, addiction, identity, and the burdens of expectation. With prose that is both razor-sharp and emotionally searing, Williams invites readers to sit with the messiness of real life — and dares them not to look away.

These are not stories that cater to ideals or sanitized portraits of womanhood. Instead, Williams presents fully realized, raw, and deeply human characters: women who curse, ache, endure, unravel, survive, and sometimes self-destruct. In stories like "Matches" and "Jesus and Jockeys," readers are drawn into the internal lives of protagonists grieving not only lost loved ones but also the disintegration of illusions: broken marriages, suffocating family roles, and childhood traumas that cling like ghosts. Each story pulses with blunt emotional honesty, delivered with a darkly humorous edge that makes even the heaviest moments achingly vivid.

Williams' greatest strength lies in her mastery of dialogue. The conversations are crisp, authentic, and often cut to the bone. Her characters speak aloud the truths many keep buried — about womanhood, resentment, domestic fatigue, and the secret costs of caregiving. Whether confronting the aftermath of a stillbirth or the silent weight of generational disappointment, the emotional resonance is piercing and true.

The title story, "The Beauty and the Hell of It," is a standout piece that captures the collection's essential message: that love and loss are inextricably intertwined, and that beauty often emerges from the things that nearly destroy us. There are no perfect endings here — only slivers of hard-won clarity, resilience in small acts, and a relentless commitment to telling the truth.

Fans of Lorrie Moore, Mary Gaitskill, and Alice Munro will find in Williams a kindred spirit. Her voice is bold, lyrical, and uncompromising. The themes she tackles are both specific and universal, grounded in the everyday yet reaching into the existential.

The Beauty and the Hell of It is a triumph of contemporary short fiction — intimate, unsettling, haunting, and profoundly resonant. Williams has crafted a collection that doesn't just reflect life — it illuminates it.

WINTER ROAD
Kristina Rienzi

Reviewer: Jeyran Main

Winter Road by Kristina Rienzi is a gripping holiday thriller that starts with heartwarming family reunions and quickly veers into chilling psychological suspense. Set in the snow-covered woods of Shady Knolls, New Jersey, this novella blends domestic drama with creeping dread, making for a unique twist on the cozy Christmas tale.

The story follows Amelia Montgomery, a successful Manhattan professional who returns home for the holidays to reconnect with her family. But her seemingly perfect life hides a dark truth—she has just broken off her engagement to the dangerously possessive Jake Grayson. When Jake shows up uninvited at her family's doorstep, what begins as awkward tension spirals into a nightmare of manipulation, stalking, and violence.

Rienzi masterfully contrasts warm holiday imagery — glowing lights, family dinners, and old flames rekindled — with an undercurrent of escalating terror. The initial scenes lull the reader into comfort before shattering it with Jake's descent into madness. Through dual perspectives, we see Jake's twisted rationale and Amelia's increasing fear, creating a tense cat-and-mouse dynamic that keeps the pages turning.

What elevates Winter Road beyond a standard suspense tale is its emotional core. Amelia's relationships with her family, particularly her vulnerable mother and protective brother, feel authentic and touching. The unexpected reappearance of Billy, her high school sweetheart, brings comfort and complication as old feelings resurface amidst the chaos. Their chemistry provides a hopeful counterbalance to the darkness surrounding them.

Jake, meanwhile, is a profoundly unsettling antagonist — charming on the surface, but seething with control and violent intent beneath. Rienzi paints his unraveling with chilling precision, making him as compelling as he is terrifying.

Paced tightly over a single Christmas Eve, the novella wastes no words. It blends thriller intensity with emotional depth, highlighting themes of control, self-worth, and the courage to confront the past. The snowy setting, once a nostalgic symbol, becomes a survival stage.

Winter Road is a fast, immersive read perfect for holiday thrillers and domestic suspense fans. It's a chilling reminder that danger can be just around the corner even in the season of peace and joy.

THE MIDNIGHT ROSE
Catalina Paris

Reviewer: Jeyran Main

The Midnight Rose by Catalina Paris is a lush, multi-threaded fantasy novel that masterfully entwines the fates of four distinct characters in a sweeping tale of magic, identity, and destiny. Drawing inspiration from classic fairy tales and the elegance of Renaissance-era worlds, this debut novel offers readers a rich, immersive escape filled with heart, intrigue, and beautifully layered storytelling.

The narrative is told through four points of view: Leo, a teenage alchemy apprentice forced to flee after a devastating attack on the Alchemical Court; Lisandre, a faerie noblewoman caught in the dangerous web of secrets within the Fey realm; Flora, a charming and spirited young witch raised on the outskirts of a mystical forest who longs to uncover the truth of her origins; and Lucien, a tormented warlock prince whose looming choices may shift the fate of his kingdom forever. Each of these characters is drawn into a shared destiny—to recover the lost Talismans of Atlantica, powerful relics that hold the key to the survival of their fractured world.

Paris's greatest strength lies in her breathtaking world-building. Every setting—from luminous faerie palaces to arcane libraries and shadowy groves—feels vivid, layered, and alive. Her attention to detail draws readers into a world where ancient magic stirs beneath political unrest, and long-buried truths are on the brink of revelation. The tone will appeal to fans of The Cruel Prince and An Enchantment of Ravens, yet the novel's mythology stands apart as something uniquely its own.

Though the early chapters introduce multiple storylines, they gradually converge with increasing momentum, culminating in a unified and emotionally satisfying narrative. The relationships are skillfully rendered, particularly the evolving bond between Lisandre and Leo, which adds depth and complexity. Flora's journey is one of bold resilience, while Lucien's struggle with inner darkness adds gravitas and moral ambiguity.

Themes of sacrifice, legacy, belonging, and the power of personal choice ripple throughout. While romance is woven into the narrative, it never overshadows the central themes or the high-stakes quest.

Paris's lyrical prose strikes a graceful balance between poetic and accessible, and her dialogue rings authentically. The Midnight Rose is a stunning debut that promises more magic and adventure to come—an enchanting beginning to what is sure to be a compelling fantasy series.

HOW TO FIND WORK FOR THE REST OF YOUR LIFE
Charles Michael Austin, ED.D.

Reviewer: Jeyran Main

In How to Find Work for the Rest of Your Life, Charles Michael Austin, ED.D., delivers a timely, empowering, and convenient guide to navigating today's ever-shifting employment landscape. As the traditional concept of long-term job security continues to fade due to forces like automation, outsourcing, globalization, and constant corporate restructuring, Austin offers insight and a clear and actionable roadmap for adapting and succeeding.

Rather than lamenting the disappearance of the lifelong career, Austin reframes the moment as a powerful opportunity for growth and reinvention. He challenges readers to shift their thinking from the outdated idea of "getting a job" to the more flexible, forward-thinking mindset of "finding work." This small language change reflects a larger, transformational perspective. In today's economy, individuals must see themselves as brands, communicating their unique value to an ever-changing market that rewards agility, creativity, and self-awareness.

The book guides readers in identifying their skills, refining their message, and presenting themselves effectively—whether they're recent graduates entering the workforce, seasoned professionals navigating a career pivot, freelancers building a business, or individuals reentering the job market later in life. Austin's strategies are practical, universally applicable, and rooted in real-world experience.

One of the book's standout qualities is its conversational and accessible tone. Rather than filling pages with jargon or academic theory, Austin writes like a mentor—direct, motivating, and easy to follow. His insights on networking, self-promotion, branding, and ongoing learning are clear and immediately usable. There's no fluff here, just valuable advice encouraging readers to control their future.

The book emphasizes the importance of lifelong learning and embracing an entrepreneurial mindset. Austin highlights adaptability, continuous skill development, and personal reinvention as core principles for building a sustainable and fulfilling work life, not just in the short term, but over the long haul.

How to Find Work for the Rest of Your Life is more than just a career manual—it's a mindset manual for the modern age. In a world where the only constant is change, Charles Michael Austin, Ed.D.'s message is empowering, practical, and essential for anyone seeking meaningful work with purpose and independence.

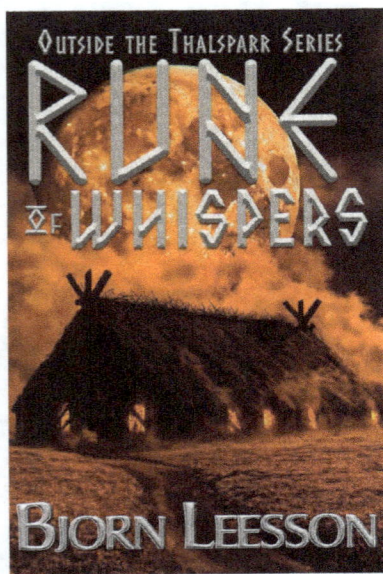

RUNE OF WHISPERS
Bjorn Leesson

Reviewer: Jeyran Main

Bjorn Leesson's Rune of Whispers, the fifth entry in the Runes of the Dokkrsdottir series, stands apart as a rich, politically charged installment that shifts the saga's focus from external warfare to internal reckoning. Trading swords for secrets and raids for whispers, this volume explores the cerebral battlegrounds of strategy, grief, diplomacy, and destiny through the eyes of Myrgjol, a Norse warrior-woman navigating Saxon politics.

Where earlier volumes brimmed with action, Rune of Whispers thrives on tension, dialogue, and emotional gravity. At its core is Myrgjol's continued evolution—not just as a leader and fighter, but as a mother, lover, and symbol of cultural adaptation. Her losses weigh heavily: her beloved Cnut is gone, and Brunhild has vanished on a vengeful quest. These absences create a backdrop of sorrow that quietly shapes her every decision.

The book excels at weaving personal narrative with political intrigue. Myrgjol must manage disputes between rival Saxon lords while maintaining autonomy for her Norse settlement. This brings external threats, like pirates and spies, and internal pressure as she questions her desires versus her responsibilities. The supporting cast—particularly the stoic Ingrid, humorous Gunndr, and the emerging Saxon-speaking allies—round out a story of community resilience and adaptation.

Leesson's writing blends Norse tradition with modern nuance, painting a deeply immersive world. Characters speak with wit and depth, and their cultural clashes and camaraderie feel both authentic and poignant. The author's skill shines especially in the dialogue and pacing, while this is a slower burn than prior volumes, the narrative feels purposeful and prosperous.

Visions, omens, and the supernatural continue to whisper through the tale, but human choices— duty versus desire, tradition versus progress—give Rune of Whispers emotional weight. Fans of Viking fiction who appreciate layered protagonists and the politics of leadership will find this installment particularly satisfying.

Ultimately, Rune of Whispers is a quiet triumph, proving that battles fought with minds and hearts can be as riveting as those fought with axes. It's a thoughtful, character-driven continuation of a deeply compelling saga.

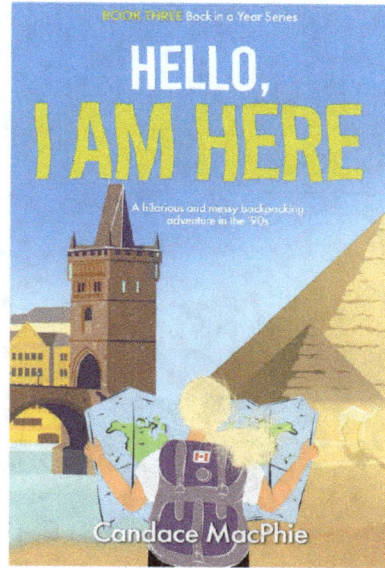

HELLO, I AM HERE
Candace MacPhie

Reviewer: Jeyran Main

Candace MacPhie's Hello, I Am Here is a beautifully candid travel memoir that dives deep into the emotional turbulence of self-discovery, grief, love, and the joy of spontaneous adventure. The third book in her Back in a Year series, this installment follows Candace as she navigates a personal detour through Europe and the Middle East — all while chasing more than just a geographic journey.

At its heart, Hello, I Am Here is about more than seeing the world. It's about showing up for yourself in the most vulnerable and exhilarating ways. MacPhie crafts a raw and intimate narrative, revealing the tension between planning and letting go, grief and healing, and between the expectations of love and the realities of independence.

The story begins in Prague, where Candace impulsively decides to reconnect with an old flame, Josh. Their chemistry, though undeniable, is complicated, and the book explores their second chance with sharp emotional insight. But the true richness of the memoir lies in her journey beyond this romantic subplot — through the streets of Munich, the deserts of Jordan, and the chaos of Cairo — where every dusty road and starlit sky holds the promise of transformation.

MacPhie writes humorously and heartily, anchoring her reflections in real-time email excerpts and journal entries. Her style is conversational, refreshingly unfiltered, and incredibly relatable. The vivid storytelling captures the grand and mundane moments of backpacking life: sleeping in cramped hostels, dealing with language barriers, bonding with fellow travelers, and confronting the internal echoes of home and loss.

Though the narrative is filled with engaging anecdotes, what lingers most is MacPhie's emotional bravery. Her grief for her mother, her longing for clarity in love, and her fierce commitment to living fully all pulse through the pages.

This memoir is not a conventional travelogue — it's a heart-on-the-sleeve chronicle of a woman reclaiming her identity in a world far from home. Hello, I Am Here is perfect for fans of Eat, Pray, Love, but with a rawer edge and a late-90s backpacker charm. It's a reminder that sometimes, you are the hardest person to find on a trip worldwide.

CAN'T RIDE AROUND IT
Ann Charles & Sam Lucky

Reviewer: Jeyran Main

Can't Ride Around It is a delightfully gritty supernatural western that balances gallows humor, heartfelt camaraderie, and ghostly thrills in the wild, wild west of 1876 Deadwood. Co-authors Ann Charles and Sam Lucky continue their Deadwood Undertaker saga with this third installment, proving once again that the series is equal parts spooky, witty, and wildly entertaining.

The story follows undertakers-turned-heroes Rabbit, Boone, and Clementine — an unlikely trio navigating the increasingly bizarre goings-on in a lawless town filled with more than just outlaws. Some secrets are buried deep, and some refuse to stay dead. The trio faces everything from vanishing corpses to walking dead and shadowy enemies raising armies with dark intentions. As the threats grow stranger, the bonds between the characters become more compelling.

Rabbit, the sharp-shooting wisecracker, brings much-needed levity to tense moments, while Boone offers a more thoughtful, steady presence. Clementine, the tough-as-nails female undertaker with a warrior's edge, remains a standout. She isn't just holding her own — she's often leading the charge, wielding weapons, investigating supernatural phenomena, and dispatching danger skillfully and stylishly.

What sets this series apart is its unique tone. It's not quite horror, entirely Western, or purely fantasy—it's a finely balanced fusion of genres. The prose is punchy and cinematic, blending old-west dialogue with modern humor. The action scenes are tightly choreographed, but what lingers most are the characters' voices, their banter, and their unexpected moments of tenderness.

The introduction of spectral Uncle Mort adds a heartfelt and humorous twist, while the escalating mystery surrounding missing bodies and necromantic forces drives the plot forward with urgency and intrigue. With references to folklore, Viking sayings, and Navajo ceremonies, the book adds cultural texture without losing its fast-paced momentum.

For readers who love their westerns weird, their horror laced with humor, and their characters rich with personality, Can't Ride Around It is a must-read. It's a rollicking, rowdy ride — full of ghostly visits, grave-digging duos, and gunfights — that reminds us the past doesn't always stay buried.

EXODUS FROM SUDAN
Alnoor Fadhl Alnoor

Reviewer: Jeyran Main

Exodus from Sudan is a moving and courageous memoir that captures both the brutal realities of political oppression and the quiet resilience of the human spirit. Alnoor Fadhl Alnoor's story begins with a stark and devastating moment. This nighttime raid shatters his family's safety and marks the beginning of a journey that will take him from the familiarity of home into a life of permanent exile. The opening pages draw readers into a deeply personal and profoundly human account set against Sudan's ongoing political turmoil.

This is more than just a narrative of escape. It is a memoir about identity, grief, longing, and reluctant transformation. At the urging of his mother, Alnoor flees Sudan as a teenager, not realizing that the separation from his homeland and family will become permanent. What follows is a harrowing and deeply emotional path through displacement, loss, and survival, leading him from temporary safety in nearby countries to a new life in the United States. Yet even in the supposed promise of a new beginning, he remains tethered to the pain of his past. His parents died before a reunion was possible, leaving wounds that never fully healed and a sense of home that remained distant and intangible.

Alnoor writes with clarity, emotional depth, and a calm, reflective tone that strengthens the impact of his experiences. His descriptions of family life in Sudan before the raid are vivid and warm, while his portrayal of grief, exile, and adaptation is honest and unflinching. What makes the memoir especially compelling is his refusal to seek pity—he offers the truth of what happened, with dignity and quiet strength.

The book is also a searing indictment of the systemic political violence that has long afflicted Sudan. Alnoor exposes the human cost of dictatorship, extremism, and state-sponsored cruelty while also illuminating the courage it takes to survive and speak out. Yet despite its tragic elements, Exodus from Sudan carries a persistent note of hope—the hope of healing, the possibility of rebuilding, and the deep yearning to remain connected to one's origins.

This is an essential and timely memoir for readers interested in human rights, refugee experiences, African politics, and personal resilience. Exodus from Sudan is a powerful testament to the endurance of the human soul in the face of unimaginable hardship.

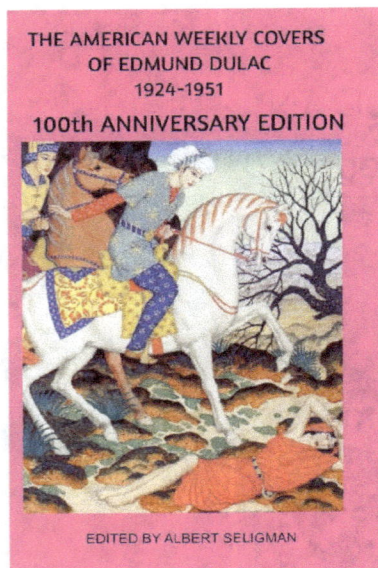

THE AMERICAN WEEKLY COVERS OF EDMUND DULAC

Albert Seligman

Reviewer: Jeyran Main

Albert Seligman's The American Weekly Covers of Edmund Dulac (100th Anniversary Edition) is a magnificent and long-overdue tribute to one of the most iconic illustrators of the Golden Age. Collecting more than one hundred cover illustrations initially created for The American Weekly between 1924 and 1951, this stunning volume revives a lesser-known but deeply significant chapter in Edmund Dulac's illustrious career, preserving, in turn, a vital piece of 20th-century visual history.

Dulac, already celebrated for his lavish fairy tale illustrations and ornate gift books, transitioned into a different realm of artistry when he began working with the Hearst Corporation. This beautifully curated edition traces that transformation, showcasing how Dulac moved from intricate fantasy illustrations to bold, streamlined compositions fit for mass-market Sunday supplements. His covers, which span biblical dramas, romantic legends, mythological sagas, and historical vignettes, are unified by his exceptional gift for visual storytelling that once captivated millions of newspaper readers.

What distinguishes this book is its dual purpose: it serves as a compelling art collection and a well-researched historical resource. Insightful notes accompany each cover on context, production, and technique. The commentary reflects a deep respect for Dulac's legacy and a dedication to scholarly accuracy. The editor openly discusses restoration efforts, detailing where digital enhancements were necessary while remaining committed to the authenticity and integrity of the original works, many of which were printed on fragile newsprint.

Seligman's introductory essay adds even more depth, offering readers a behind-the-scenes look at Dulac's creative process and the evolving print technologies of the time. From early challenges with color reproduction to later breakthroughs in layout and design, the narrative provides a deeper understanding of how Dulac skillfully adapted his vision to the commercial print world. Highlights of the collection include Dulac's vivid Bible series, the iconic "Famous Vamps of History," and the enchanting fairy tale–themed covers—all restored with remarkable clarity and vibrancy.

Beyond its aesthetic and academic value, the book tells a broader cultural story of changing tastes, media evolution, and the tension between fine art and popular publishing. For illustrators, historians, collectors, and enthusiasts of narrative art, this edition is more than a nostalgic reprint; it is a reclaiming of forgotten genius.

With elegance, reverence, and depth, The American Weekly Covers of Edmund Dulac is a must-have for any serious lover of art, illustration, or visual storytelling.

IGNITION
Alexander Alten

Reviewer: Jeyran Main

Strap in — Ignition is a high-stakes techno-thriller where biotech, ambition, and betrayal converge in a world that feels eerily one decision away from our own. Alexander Alten's debut novel marks the explosive beginning of what is set to be a five-part series, and from the very first page, it grips you with a razor-sharp intensity and refuses to let go.

Set in a near-future landscape shaped by rapid technological progress and political corruption, Ignition immerses readers in a tangled web of corporate espionage, covert alliances, and unapologetically complex characters. Alten crafts a universe where trust is scarce and survival depends not on brute strength but cunning, resilience, and a willingness to outthink the game. Central to this narrative are powerful female protagonists who do not play by conventional rules— they break them and rebuild the system in their image. These women are brilliant, unpredictable, and undeniably dangerous, and they challenge every assumption of what it means to lead, to fight, and to win.

What truly distinguishes Ignition is the tension that pulses through its core, not just between factions and rivals, but within the characters themselves. Alten's world is filled with moral ambiguity, where motivations are rarely pure, and every alliance carries the threat of betrayal. Readers are drawn into this maze of uncertainty, questioning loyalties and second-guessing choices at every turn. It's that sense of constant unease that makes the novel so compelling.

Despite its futuristic premise, the story is grounded in current fears—biotech surveillance, corporate overreach, and unchecked ambition. Alten's portrayal of innovation is rooted in real scientific potential, sidestepping sci-fi clichés in favor of plausible advancements with terrifying consequences. The political implications are chilling, echoing contemporary anxieties about power, privacy, and control.

The novel's pacing is relentless yet refined. Action scenes are executed precisely, while dialogue crackles with subtext and layered intent. Alten's prose is confident, clear, and unapologetically bold, blending the grit of a modern thriller with the speculative bite of classic dystopian fiction.

For fans of Killing Eve, Orphan Black, or the politically charged works of Michael Crichton, Ignition delivers on every front. It doesn't merely introduce a story—it launches a world, characters, and conflicts that demand attention. This is not just a promising debut—it's a signal flare, a call to buckle in and prepare for the ride ahead.

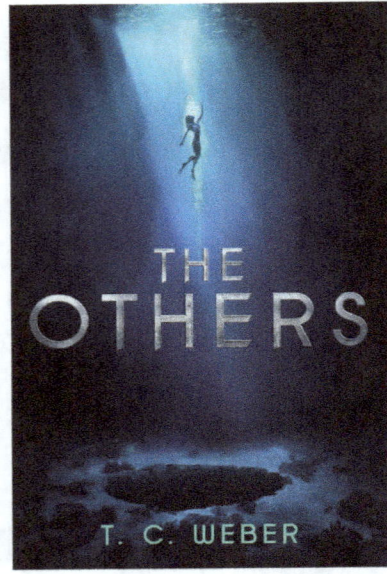

THE OTHERS
T. C. Weber

Reviewer: Jeyran Main

T. C. Weber's The Others is a genre-blending triumph—equal parts eco-thriller, speculative science fiction, and unconventional romance. It begins with a storm and a body: one washed ashore during a hurricane, with webbed feet and aquatic features that defy explanation. When marine biologist Will Myers is called in to assist, he's pulled into a mystery that's far deeper than the sea itself.

The plot quickly dives into uncharted waters, both literally and figuratively. Will meets Andreia, the enigmatic sister of the deceased, and soon discovers a hidden undersea civilization—one built not by humans, but by an endangered aquatic species forced into the shadows by rising seas, disease, and centuries of human destruction. It's a bold premise, but Weber pulls it off with grace and gravity.

What elevates The Others is its emotional core. Will and Andreia's relationship feels delicate and organic, anchored in grief, hope, and a shared mission to heal a fractured planet. Their connection adds depth to the environmental narrative, making the stakes feel personal and global.

Weber's worldbuilding is immersive without being heavy-handed. The undersea society is a fascinating mix of outcasts and rebels—hackers, smugglers, and idealists clinging to survival beneath the surface of a hostile world. The pacing is tight, the tension builds naturally, and the mystery surrounding Andreia's brother's death is a compelling spine to the story.

But at its heart, The Others is a cautionary tale. It explores humanity's long-standing estrangement from the ocean and the cascading consequences of that neglect. Weber doesn't lecture—he dramatizes. The book examines environmental collapse, xenophobia, and the cost of secrecy while delivering a gripping and heartfelt narrative.

This novel strikes a similar chord for fans of The Shape of Water, Annihilation, or The Abyss. It merges ecological urgency with the mystery of the unknown and the complexities of cross-species empathy. It's intimate and sweeping, speculative and grounded.

T. C. Weber has crafted a story that resonates on multiple levels: as a romance, a thriller, and a rallying cry for the oceans we're losing. The Others is a compelling call to look deeper at our world, actions, and what it means to belong truly.

TALES OF THE FORTHCOMING
Steven Blows

Reviewer: Jeyran Main

What does the future hold — wonder or terror, love or loss, progress or peril? In Steven Blows' imaginative and daring anthology Tales of the Forthcoming, the answer is all of the above, delivered through ten distinct short stories that span science fiction, the supernatural, and the profoundly human. This collection dares to ask big questions while offering the wit, suspense, and emotional resonance defining great speculative storytelling.

Each story stands confidently on its own, yet the collection is thematically unified by its curiosity about the future and the evolution or deterioration of the human spirit under extraordinary circumstances. From planetary politics' chaos to artificial intelligence's loneliness, Blows captures what it means to be alive in imagined tomorrows. Stories like "The Orb of King Wallace" offer high-stakes tomb-raiding thrills laced with sci-fi wonder and a haunting twist. "Mezameru" provides a quieter, more contemplative piece that probes synthetic consciousness and emerging emotional awareness. Then there's "Family Dinner & Troubling Times" — a comedic yet biting tale of cross-species family dynamics that will resonate with anyone who's ever survived an awkward holiday meal.

Blows' strength lies in his genre-blending. Horror flirts with satire, and tender drama runs parallel to dystopian thrillers. His narrative voice is flexible, adapting seamlessly to each story's needs while maintaining a consistent creative spark throughout the collection. This versatility makes Tales of the Forthcoming feel like a diverse, vibrant, and unpredictable galaxy.

Despite the range in tone, the anthology is more than just an exercise in imagination. Blows dives into themes of grief, identity, ambition, and connection, giving emotional weight to the speculative settings. Even amid alien technologies and post-human societies, the reader is always tethered to something tangible — love, regret, hope, fear. The stories move quickly but leave a lasting impact, often concluding with abrupt, thought-provoking endings. Some bring closure; others leave a quiet unease.

Fans of Black Mirror, Ray Bradbury, or Neal Shusterman's speculative fiction will find much to savor here. Blows balances heady concepts with sharp wit and a storyteller's heart. His anthology isn't just about what might come — it's about who we might become.

So, as the author himself suggests, make a cuppa and dive in. You'll finish Tales of the Forthcoming entertained, challenged, and perhaps more introspective about the strange road ahead.

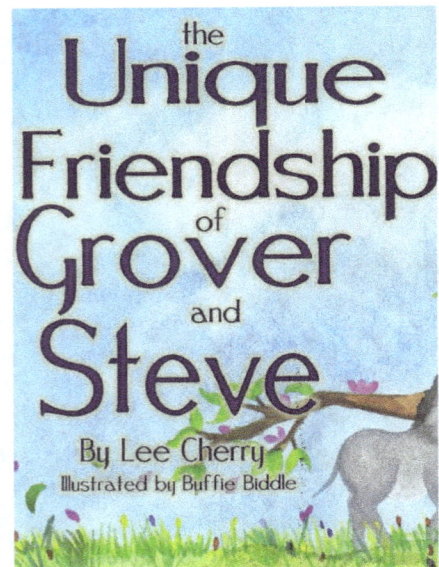

THE UNIQUE FRIENDSHIP OF GROVER & STEVE

Lee Cherry

Reviewer: Jeyran Main

In The Unique Friendship of Grover & Steve, Lee Cherry delivers a charming and heartfelt tale that resonates deeply with readers of all ages. Set against the sweeping openness of the Great Plains, this beautifully illustrated children's book tells the story of two unlikely companions—Grover, a kind-hearted donkey, and Steve, a curious ostrich—who form an unexpected yet unshakable bond. It's a gentle yet profound reminder that true friendship transcends appearances, habits, and expectations.

The idea of a donkey and an ostrich becoming best friends with the other animals on the plains seems laughable. They're different in every observable way—body, behavior, and background. But Grover and Steve are undeterred. They don't let outward differences define their connection. Instead, they build their friendship on loyalty, support, and shared joy. Through their journey, readers learn that the most enduring relationships are built not on similarity but mutual care and understanding.

Lee Cherry uses this unique pairing to deliver timely and timeless lessons about diversity, inclusion, and empathy. The narrative gently challenges preconceived notions about who we're "supposed" to connect with and encourages children to look beyond the surface. It invites readers to celebrate individuality, rather than fear it. The book communicates these themes in an age-appropriate and emotionally resonant way, making it a perfect read for children, parents, and educators alike.

The prose is engaging and straightforward, designed with young readers in mind, yet it contains layers of meaning that adults will also appreciate. The wide, open setting of the Great Plains mirrors the story's emotional landscape, symbolizing the freedom to choose your path—and your friends—regardless of what others may think.

This is more than a sweet animal story. It's a subtle, powerful message wrapped in a delightful tale that can spark meaningful conversations about kindness, respect, and inclusivity. The Unique Friendship of Grover & Steve offers a refreshing perspective on unity and acceptance in a world that often emphasizes division.

Whether read aloud in a classroom, shared during bedtime, or given as a thoughtful gift, this story offers something meaningful for every reader. With its endearing characters and uplifting message, Lee Cherry's book will become a treasured part of many children's early literary journeys—a gentle but firm reminder that friendship knows no bounds.

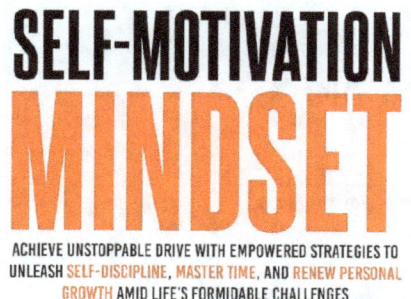

SELF—MOTIVATION MINDSET
Laurie James

Reviewer: Jeyran Main

In a world where burnout, imposter syndrome, and constant pressure seem the new normal, Laurie James's Self-Motivation Mindset is a timely, empowering, and refreshingly practical guide for high-achievers looking to reclaim their inner drive. This isn't just another motivational book filled with clichés —it's a well-researched, experience-backed manual for real change.

From the first page, James clarifies that this book is not about surface-level inspiration. Instead, it digs deep into the psychology and science behind motivation, combining actionable tools with relatable stories and simple, impactful exercises. Whether you're a business leader, healthcare professional, student, or someone navigating a high-stress career, Self-Motivation Mindset is tailored to meet you where you are — and push you further.

The book's structure is deliberate and focused. It begins with identifying what truly drives you and leads into strategies for managing stress, breaking through limiting beliefs, and transforming failure into opportunity. What sets this guide apart is how it blends neuroscience and self-help into something usable. It's not about lofty ideals but about proven strategies you can implement immediately — from time management methods that reduce burnout to mindfulness techniques that enhance clarity and focus.

Standout chapters include practical solutions for tackling imposter syndrome, shifting from external validation to internal motivation, and embracing lifelong learning as a tool for resilience. The tone is encouraging without being patronizing, and James's writing balances empathy with expertise — like a coach who's been through it all and knows just when to push and when to reassure.

What's especially refreshing is the book's recognition that motivation isn't one-size-fits-all. Readers are guided to reflect and adapt strategies based on their goals, challenges, and values.

If you've ever found yourself stuck in the cycle of "high performance followed by exhaustion," this book is for you. If you've read other self-help books that felt disconnected from reality, Self-Motivation Mindset will feel like a breath of fresh air.

Laurie James delivers a grounded, intelligent, and empowering call to action: Your motivation doesn't come from the outside—it lives within you. You need to know how to unlock it.

RUNNIN' NO MORE
G.T. DÍPÈ

Reviewer: Jeyran Main

Runnin' No More by G.T. DÍPÈ is a profoundly affecting and emotionally layered novel that explores love, identity, trauma, and the quiet strength required to stop fleeing from one's own pain. With lyrical restraint and poignant clarity, DÍPÈ presents a moving portrait of two men on parallel journeys — not just of migration, but of emotional reckoning.

Teniade Adeowo is a Nigerian man fleeing more than one country. Carrying the invisible scars of a society that criminalizes who he is, Ade leaves for England not in search of freedom, but of invisibility. Haunted by legal threats and emotional wounds, he lands in Heathrow with hopes of anonymity. Stefan Wickström, a Swede with his own heavy past, believes that staying in constant motion is the only way to avoid confronting his inner turmoil. When the two meet in the transient space of an airport, what begins is not a whirlwind romance but a quiet, cautious connection rooted in mutual recognition and pain.

What unfolds in Runnin' No More is not simply a love story, though love is at its heart in all its complexity. DÍPÈ crafts a narrative of slow trust, honest vulnerability, and the courage to stand still long enough to be known. The prose is gentle yet penetrating, allowing the characters to speak through silence as much as through dialogue. Readers are invited to linger in their shared moments, to witness the ebb and flow of fear, desire, and hope.

The novel is also a sharp commentary on the intersections of queerness, displacement, and systemic injustice. Ade's narrative highlights the lived reality of LGBTQ+ individuals in places where their existence is criminalized. Stefan, while protected by Western freedoms, grapples with internalized trauma that no border crossing can erase. Together, their relationship becomes a fragile space of refuge — imperfect but real.

DÍPÈ does not indulge in melodrama; instead, she offers a profoundly human story that resonates with quiet power. Her writing is graced even in the rawest moments, and its depth lingers long after the final page.

This novel will feel familiar in emotional weight for readers of Call Me by Your Name, A Little Life, or The Prophets, but DÍPÈ's voice and cultural lens offer something wholly original. Runnin' No More is a tender and necessary story about love, stillness, and the reclamation of self when running is no longer an option.

A SMALL COMPASS
Cinda Gault

Reviewer: Jeyran Main

In a literary canon long dominated by male voices, Cinda Gault's A Small Compass is a breath of fierce, fresh air — a poetic reclamation of two women history nearly forgot. Set against the vast, unforgiving backdrop of early 19th-century Canada, the novel is both a stirring tale of endurance and a powerful meditation on agency, survival, and the tenacity of the female spirit.

The story follows Isobel Gunn and Marie-Anne Gaboury, the first non-Indigenous women to enter the Canadian western frontier. Gault gives voice to these historical figures with grace and grit, illuminating the lives they led beyond the footnotes of colonial records. Isobel, born on Orkney Island — dubbed the "Island of Women" due to the absence of men — chafes under the limits of domestic life. In bold defiance, she disguises herself as a man to join the Hudson's Bay Company, refusing to accept a future dictated by societal expectations. Marie-Anne, meanwhile, follows her fur-trader husband into the unknown, torn between devotion and the gnawing fear of isolation, hardship, and widowhood.

Their stories converge in the harsh wilderness, where snow, hunger, and loneliness press in from all sides. Yet what emerges is not a tale of conquest, but of resilience — a raw and beautiful portrait of two women forging identity and companionship in a world that renders them invisible.

Gault's prose is lyrical yet grounded, drawing readers deep into the landscape without losing sight of the emotional terrain. Each woman's inner world is richly rendered, revealing their struggles, quiet triumphs, and fragile hopes. The pacing mirrors their journey — deliberate, enduring, and ultimately transformative. Gault avoids melodrama in favor of something more powerful: honesty.

At its core, A Small Compass is a feminist work, though never in a didactic way. It portrays the realities of gender, colonial hardship, and survival with clarity and nuance. These are not heroines plucked from legend — they are real, flawed, and unforgettable. The wilderness does not yield easily to them, but they do not bend. They endure.

A Small Compass will resonate deeply for readers who enjoy historical fiction with depth, beauty, and a sharp social conscience, such as The Outlander series, The Luminaries, or Circe. It is a quiet, courageous novel that rewrites the margins of history and honors the untold lives of women who dared to walk off the map.

WYVERN (DARK LAIR TRILOGY: BOOK ONE)

D. J. O'Brien

Reviewer: Jeyran Main

D. J. O'Brien's Wyvern is a sweeping epic that plunges readers into a richly built medieval fantasy world, where shadows stir and destinies collide. As the first installment in the Dark Lair Trilogy, this novel sets the stage for a high-stakes saga of power, prophecy, and peril, perfect for fans of traditional heroic fantasy.

The novel opens with a classic yet compelling premise: a princess abducted, a rescue party assembled, and ancient forces awakening beneath the surface of human conflict. But O'Brien doesn't stop there. A multilayered tale unfolds through multiple perspectives, weaving together threads of personal identity, political unrest, and looming supernatural evil.

At the center is Brinn Thronso, a man of unknown lineage raised by nuns, whose search for truth about his origins becomes a journey of both self-discovery and world-altering consequence. Brinn is joined by a diverse cast of characters — soldiers, royalty, rebels — each bringing unique depth and emotional stakes to the narrative. O'Brien's use of multiple POVs is deftly handled, enriching the worldbuilding and lending complexity to every plot turn.

What elevates Wyvern is its thematic depth. While the story is driven by classic good-versus-evil tension, it's not just about external enemies. The novel explores betrayal, legacy, and the moral gray areas even in fantasy's most archetypal roles. The threat of the dark god Badur, imprisoned but far from defeated, looms large — and the ancient crystals and royal bloodlines needed to seal him away again add mythic urgency to the quest.

Pacing is brisk but deliberate. With 469 pages, there's ample room for O'Brien to establish a detailed world, from the warring human factions to the desolate wilds of Gantu, where slavers and warlords wage their dark games. The lore is profound but accessible, and the writing stays grounded even during magical or political exposition.

Wyvern is a compelling start to a trilogy that promises high fantasy stakes with classic storytelling heart. For readers who miss the likes of David Eddings, Raymond E. Feist, or Terry Brooks, this is a world well worth venturing into.

ABUNDANCE
Alan Chan

Reviewer: Jeyran Main

Abundance is an intelligent, sharp-edged space thriller that rockets you from corporate boardrooms to international intrigue, all through the eyes of a reluctant hero long past his glory days.

Charles "Chuck" Sorrel, a former astronaut turned jaded consultant, is brought in to investigate a fatal disaster involving the first commercial asteroid mining mission. What starts as a paper-pushing gig quickly spirals into a global power play when a rival Chinese company, Yangshen, becomes entangled in the fallout. With tension mounting, Sorrel is dragged far beyond his comfort zone — from quiet interviews to high-stakes dinners, tense encounters with grieving loved ones, and a geopolitical storm that refuses to settle.

What makes Abundance shine is its grounded realism and dry wit. Chuck is the protagonist who doesn't ask for adventure but ends up in it anyway, equipped with little more than cynicism and reluctant determination. He's not your typical space cowboy — more like a weary gumshoe in zero gravity. The book leans into this noir tone while wrapping it in near-future tech and socio-political complexity that feels unsettlingly plausible.

The pacing is tight. Each chapter moves with purpose, slowly peeling back layers of corporate secrets and moral ambiguity. The dialogue is natural, often tinged with sarcasm, and the worldbuilding, particularly around space commercialization, is handled with impressive subtlety. There's no info-dumping here; you're dropped in and expected to keep up, which adds to the book's overall intelligence.

Yet for all the suspense and scandal, Abundance never loses sight of its emotional core. Sorrel isn't just solving a mystery — he's grappling with loss, legacy, and the long shadows of his past. His interactions with Jen, the Mission Commander's widow, are some of the most poignant moments in the book, reminding you that even in a story of orbital politics, humanity always stays center stage.

This novel is for readers who enjoy Michael Crichton's tech thrillers, but want them laced with world-weary humor and a touch more soul. Competent, timely, and surprisingly moving — Abundance lives up to its name.